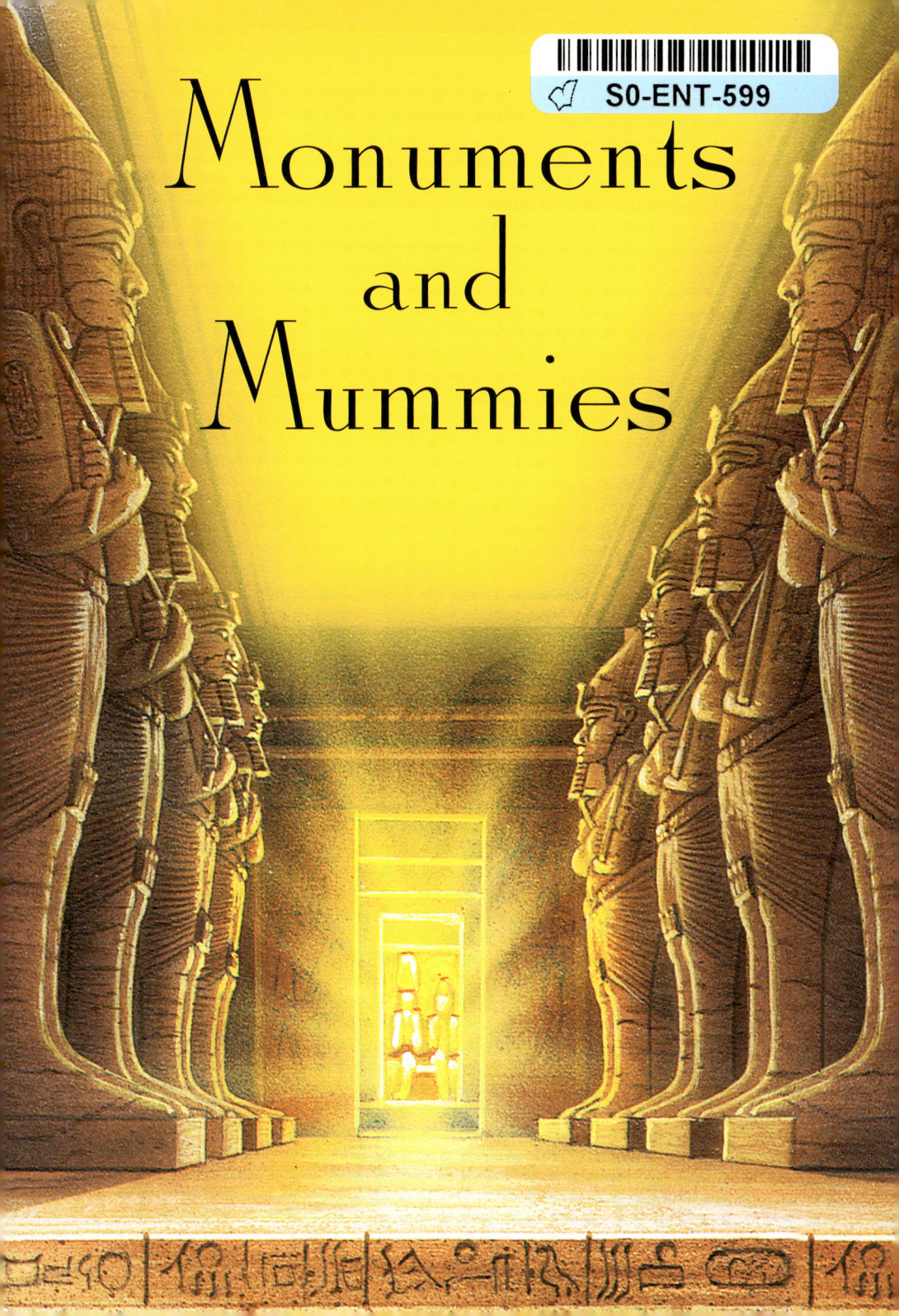

Contents

An Ancient World	4
The Power of the Pharaohs	6
The Royal Role	8
Egyptian Style	10
Mighty Monuments	12
The Pyramid Builders	14
Under Wraps	16
The Mummy Makers	18
Tombs of Treasure	20
Riddles in Stone	22
An Ancient Art	24
Keeping the Past Alive	26
The Secret Chamber	28
Glossary	30
Index	31
Research Starters	32

Features

Do you know that the ancient Greeks and Romans visited the pyramids of Egypt as tourists? Turn to page 13 to learn more.

The pyramid builders may have worked with simple tools, but they were extremely exact in their measurements. Discover more on page 15.

Ancient artifacts weren't always treated with respect. Read **Mistreated Mummies?** on page 17 and see what you think about history in danger.

Adventure awaits! Follow the clues on page 28 to find your way through ancient Egypt and discover the treasure in **The Secret Chamber**.

Who was Cleopatra?
Visit **www.rigbyinfoquest.com**
for more about **ANCIENT EGYPT**.

An Ancient World

For thousands of years, people have made homes, raised animals, and grown crops on the fertile land along the banks of the mighty River Nile. The river cuts through the stony desert land of Northern Africa in an area we know today as Egypt. Each year, the River Nile flooded its banks, covering the nearby land with thick, dark mud that later became rich soil. Food was plentiful and life was good for many people who lived there.

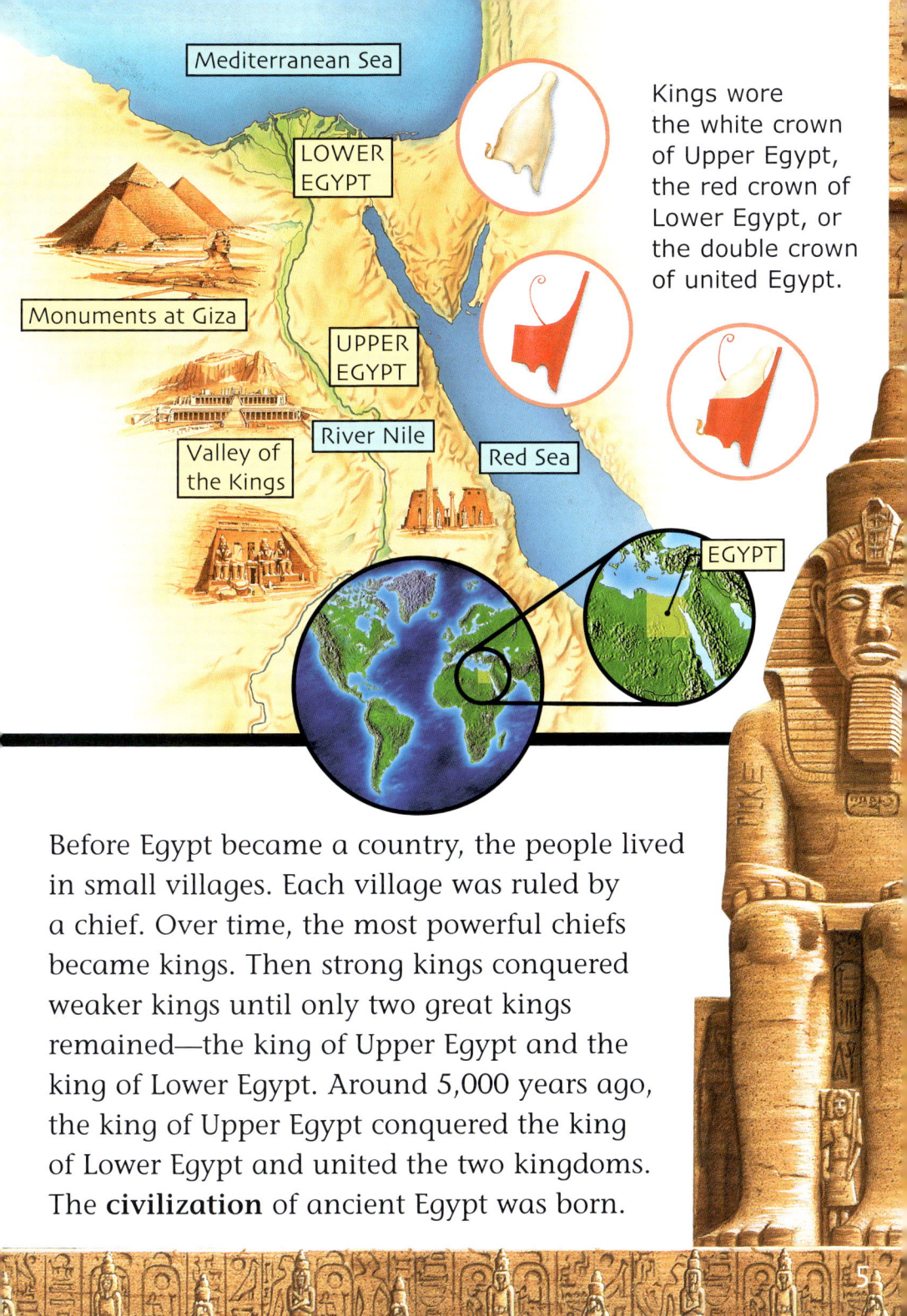

Kings wore the white crown of Upper Egypt, the red crown of Lower Egypt, or the double crown of united Egypt.

Before Egypt became a country, the people lived in small villages. Each village was ruled by a chief. Over time, the most powerful chiefs became kings. Then strong kings conquered weaker kings until only two great kings remained—the king of Upper Egypt and the king of Lower Egypt. Around 5,000 years ago, the king of Upper Egypt conquered the king of Lower Egypt and united the two kingdoms. The **civilization** of ancient Egypt was born.

The Power of the Pharaohs

Powerful kings called **pharaohs** ruled ancient Egypt for more than 3,000 years. The pharaohs made Egypt a strong and wealthy nation. They ordered the building of massive monuments, magnificent temples, and towering tombs. They employed architects and engineers to build great cities, and teams of skilled craftspeople to make beautiful objects and fine jewelry.

The Egyptian people believed a pharaoh was a king of the gods. Sons inherited the throne from their fathers, and the time that a ruling family stayed in power was known as a **dynasty**. The ancient Egyptian civilization lasted for thirty Egyptian dynasties and two Greek dynasties before it fell to the Romans. It is the longest running empire in history.

The dynasties of the pharaohs are divided into three main periods—the Old Kingdom, the Middle Kingdom, and the New Kingdom.

The royal family often displayed its power and wealth during ceremonies, processions, and visits to temples.

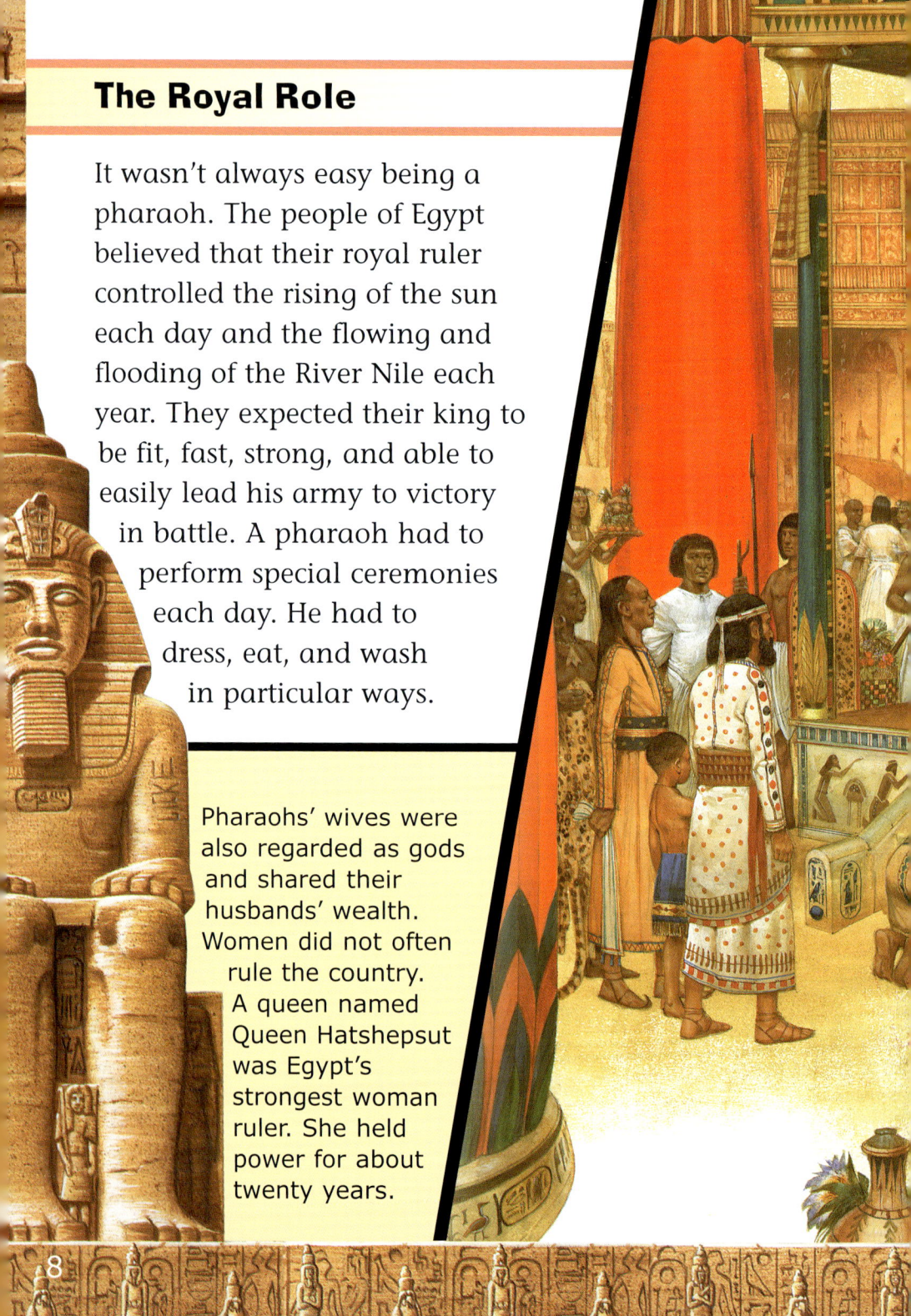

The Royal Role

It wasn't always easy being a pharaoh. The people of Egypt believed that their royal ruler controlled the rising of the sun each day and the flowing and flooding of the River Nile each year. They expected their king to be fit, fast, strong, and able to easily lead his army to victory in battle. A pharaoh had to perform special ceremonies each day. He had to dress, eat, and wash in particular ways.

Pharaohs' wives were also regarded as gods and shared their husbands' wealth. Women did not often rule the country. A queen named Queen Hatshepsut was Egypt's strongest woman ruler. She held power for about twenty years.

The Power of the Pharaohs continued

Even a pharaoh could not keep peace and power without help, however. Ancient Egyptian society was organized so that government ministers, officials, scribes, and priests also held positions of leadership. Craftspeople held a lower place in society, and the peasants who worked the land and built the royal tombs and temples were the largest, but least powerful, part of the population.

Egyptian Style

All ancient Egyptians, from pharaohs to peasants, liked to look good. People dressed in white linen clothing, and both men and women wore makeup and jewelry. Egyptians used perfumed oils to protect their skin from the harsh desert winds. Hair was an important feature, and many Egyptians wore stylish wigs. At banquets, women often wore scented cones of wax that released perfume as the wax melted over their wigs and clothes!

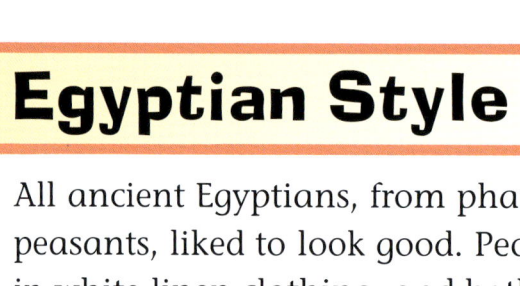

Outdoor markets, called bazaars, are found to this day in the old sections of Egyptian cities and towns.

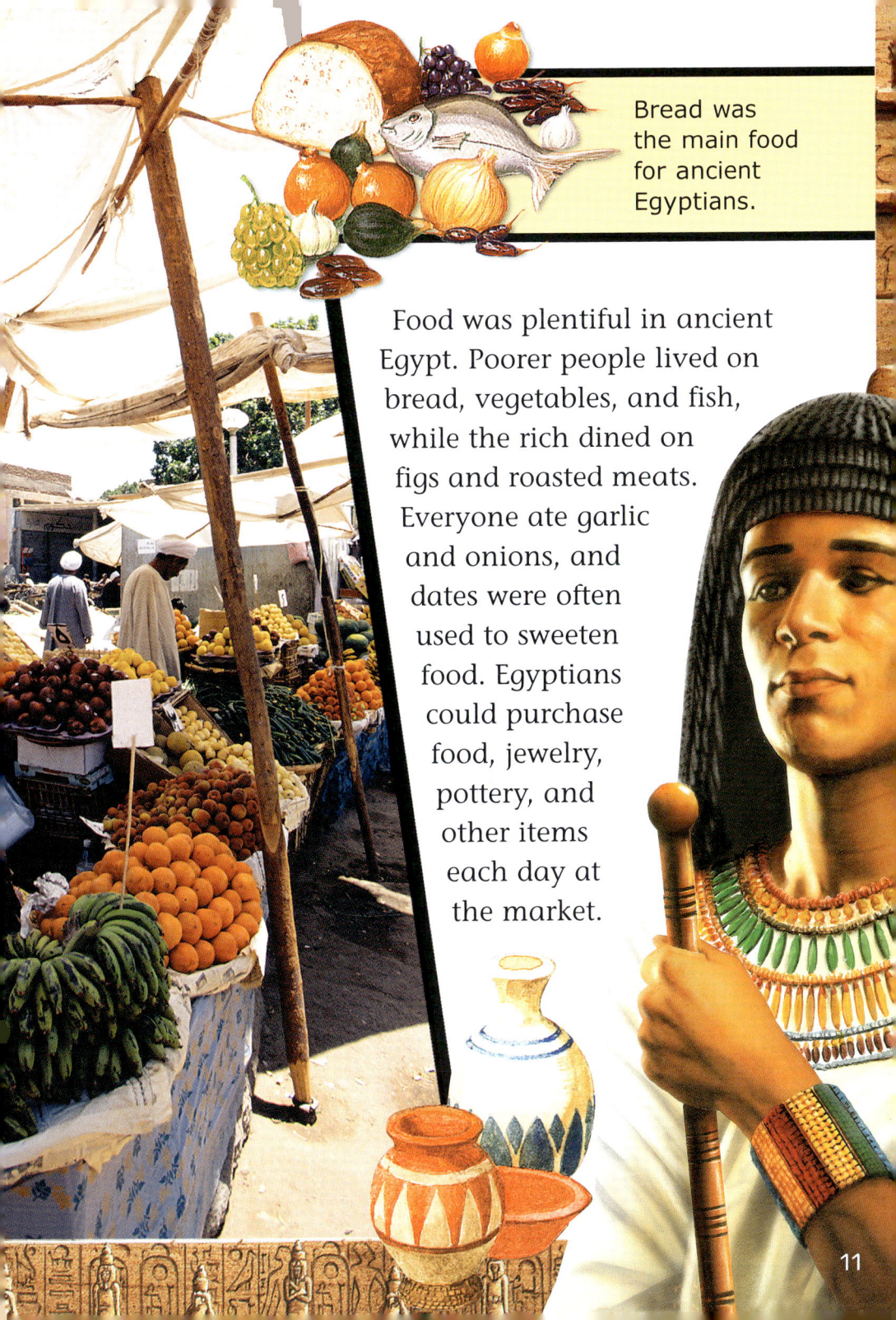

Bread was the main food for ancient Egyptians.

Food was plentiful in ancient Egypt. Poorer people lived on bread, vegetables, and fish, while the rich dined on figs and roasted meats. Everyone ate garlic and onions, and dates were often used to sweeten food. Egyptians could purchase food, jewelry, pottery, and other items each day at the market.

Mighty Monuments

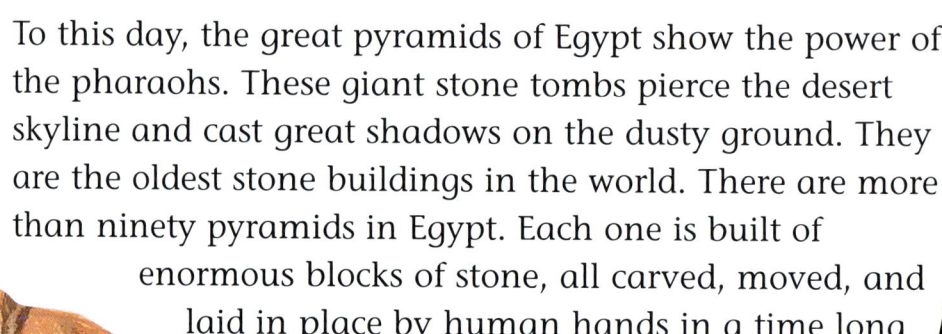

To this day, the great pyramids of Egypt show the power of the pharaohs. These giant stone tombs pierce the desert skyline and cast great shadows on the dusty ground. They are the oldest stone buildings in the world. There are more than ninety pyramids in Egypt. Each one is built of enormous blocks of stone, all carved, moved, and laid in place by human hands in a time long before high-tech tools and machinery.

Over the years, moisture, wind, and sandstorms have worn away the pyramids so that what we see today are just their cores. Experts believe that the Great Pyramids at Giza may have been capped with gold and covered in highly polished stones that glittered and gleamed in the sun.

A giant statue of a sphinx—a creature with the head and intelligence of a human but the body and strength of a lion—guards the pyramids at Giza. It was a symbol of royal power.

TIME LINK

The Greek historian and writer Herodotus visited the pyramids 2,000 years after they were built. His writings encouraged the ancient Greeks and Romans to visit the monuments of Egypt as tourists. Even during their time, the monuments were thought to be ancient. Today, thousands of tourists visit these wonders of the ancient world.

When the pyramids were built at Giza, they were surrounded by desert. Today, the suburbs of Cairo are creeping closer to them.

The Pyramid Builders

The ordinary citizens of Egypt built the pyramids. Each pyramid project was started when a pharaoh came to power and stopped when he died. It took expert skills and a massive workforce to build a pyramid. Astronomers studied the stars to determine the best site, architects and mathematicians took measurements, masons shaped blocks of stone, and overseers organized teams of several thousand workers.

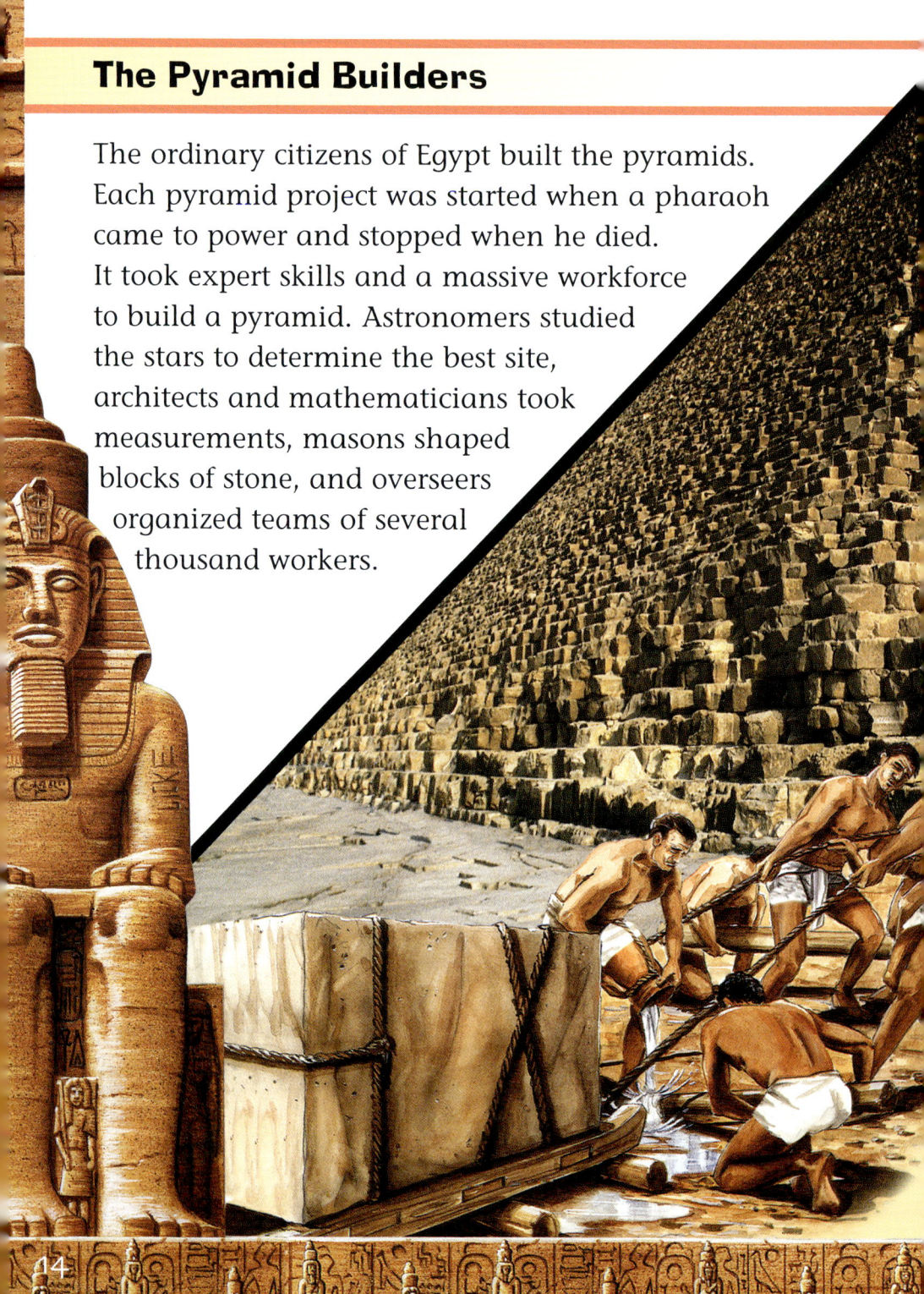

Mighty Monuments continued

When a pharaoh died, his body was placed in a burial chamber deep inside the core of a pyramid. The ancient Egyptians believed that one day the world would end, and at that time they would move on to another life. A pyramid was a special waiting place. A pharaoh was buried with all the treasures he might need in the next life.

Experts believe that it took about 20,000 to 30,000 workers to cut the great stone blocks from the quarries, transport the blocks to the building sites, and build the pyramids. The building measurements of the pyramids are exact. The outer stone slabs of the Great Pyramid fit so tightly that even a hair cannot be pushed between them.

Under Wraps

To the ancient Egyptians, the human body was one of the most important things that a person needed to move on to the afterlife. Poor people were buried in the desert where the scorching heat sometimes dried and preserved their bodies in the sand. Wealthy people could afford to have their bodies preserved as mummies and placed with their most treasured possessions in special tombs.

Mummified bodies were wrapped in layers of linen bandages. They were laid inside specially carved or painted cases, which were then placed inside **sarcophagi** to protect them from tomb raiders or wild animals.

The mummy shown at right is that of Ramses II, a famous pharaoh who ruled from 1290 to 1224 B.C. It is on display in the museum of Cairo, Egypt.

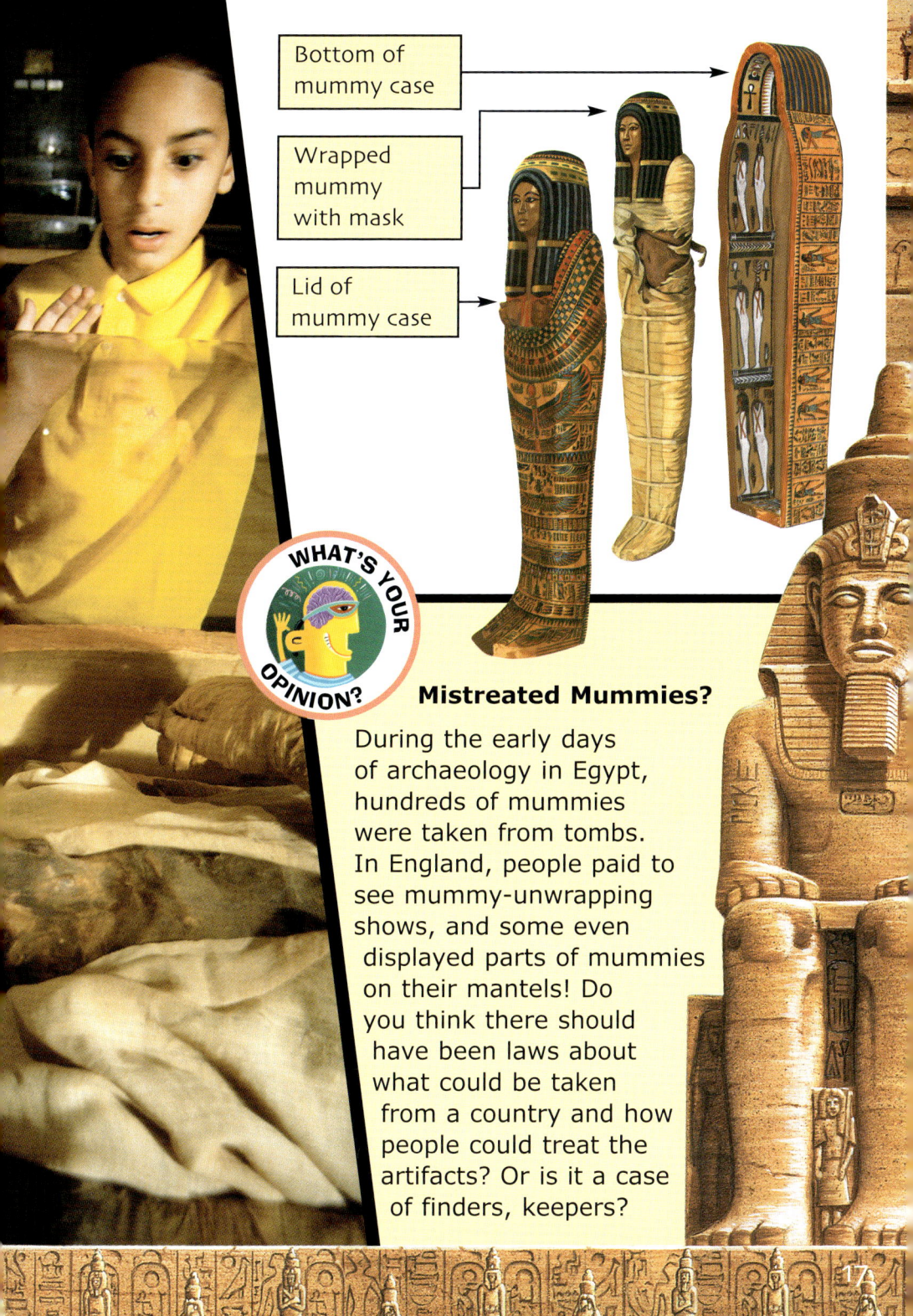

Bottom of mummy case

Wrapped mummy with mask

Lid of mummy case

WHAT'S YOUR OPINION?

Mistreated Mummies?

During the early days of archaeology in Egypt, hundreds of mummies were taken from tombs. In England, people paid to see mummy-unwrapping shows, and some even displayed parts of mummies on their mantels! Do you think there should have been laws about what could be taken from a country and how people could treat the artifacts? Or is it a case of finders, keepers?

The Mummy Makers

People who made dead bodies into mummies were called **embalmers**. It was their job to dry out a body to prevent it from rotting. Techniques changed over time, but most embalmers removed the brain, liver, lungs, stomach, and intestines and stored them in **canopic jars**, which would later be placed in the tomb. They then washed the body and covered it in **natron** to soak up any moisture.

After forty days, the embalmers rubbed the skin with oils or resins and stuffed the body with spices, linen, and sawdust to reshape it. They wrapped the body in layers of linen bandages, placing charms and jewelry between the strips.

After a total of seventy days, the mummy was sealed in its case. The mummy's face was often covered with a mask before it was placed in the tomb.

Under Wraps continued

The ancient Egyptians believed that cats were sacred. When a pet cat died, the owners would shave off their eyebrows in mourning. Ancient Egyptians often mummified their cats so that they would see them in the next life.

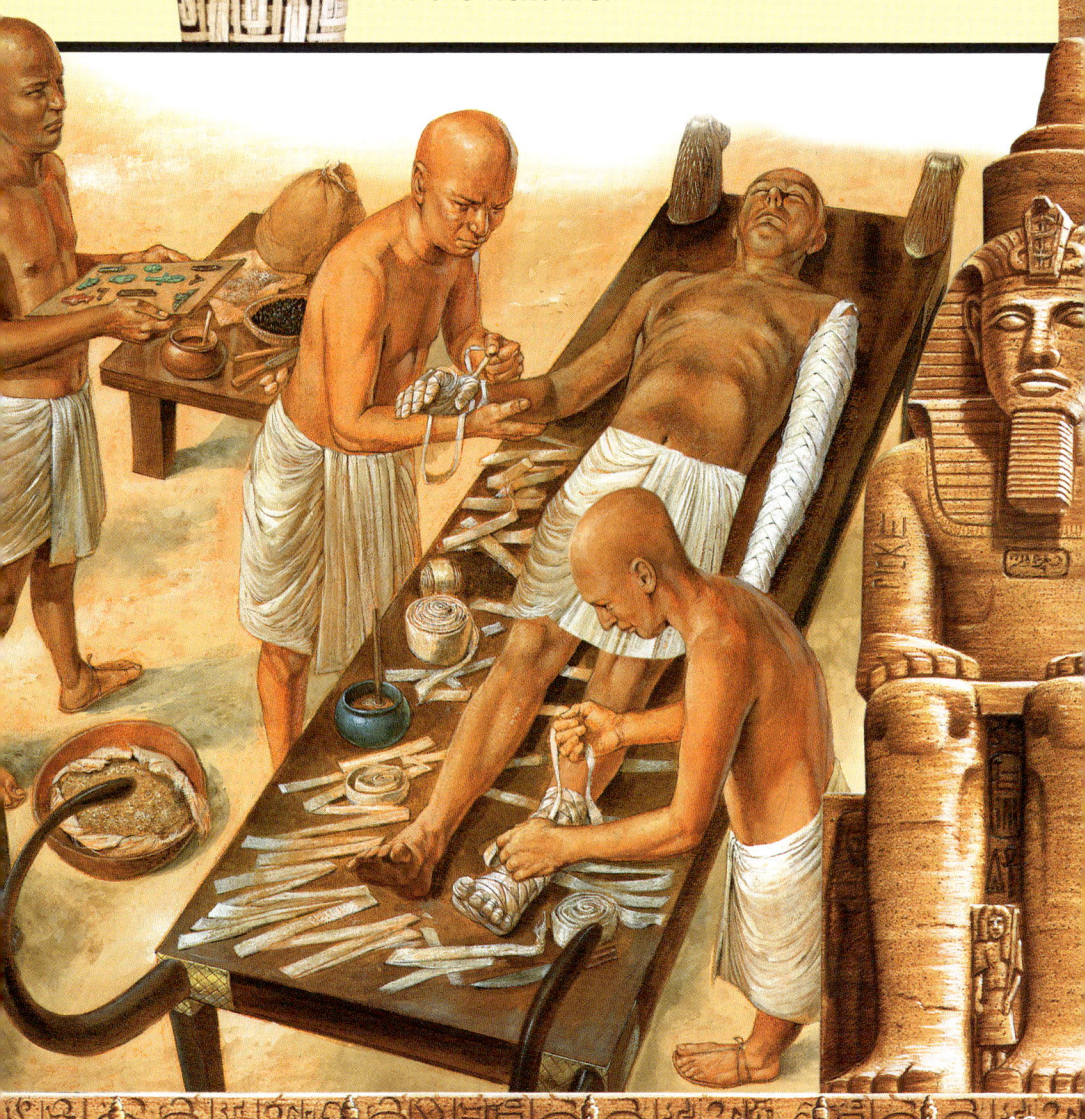

Tombs of Treasure

The mummies of the pharaohs were buried deep within pyramids, in secret chambers filled with precious gems, glittering gold, and other treasures. Every ancient Egyptian, including thieves, knew that the pyramids were packed full of tempting treasures. All but one of the burial chambers we know about were robbed before the end of ancient Egyptian civilization.

A boy-king named Tutankhamen became the world's most famous mummy when his hidden tomb was discovered by an English **Egyptologist** named Howard Carter, in 1922. King Tutankhamen's tomb had not been opened in 3,000 years. His mummified body was sealed within three beautiful cases, the last one made of solid gold. A glittering golden mask covered the face of the mummy.

It took Carter ten years to search and catalog the contents of the tomb. He found jewels and gold thrones, chariots, statues, swords, and shields.

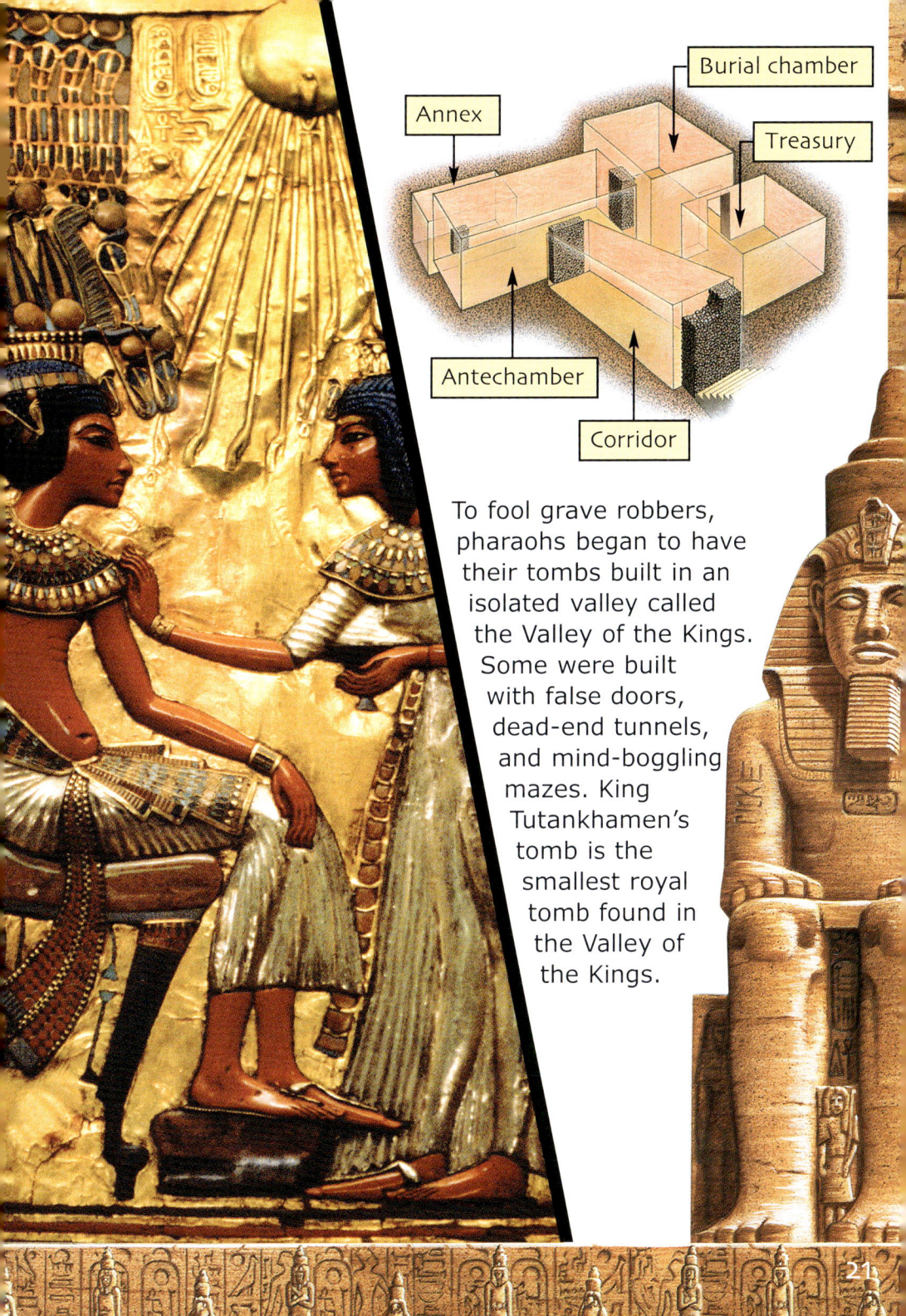

Burial chamber
Annex
Treasury
Antechamber
Corridor

To fool grave robbers, pharaohs began to have their tombs built in an isolated valley called the Valley of the Kings. Some were built with false doors, dead-end tunnels, and mind-boggling mazes. King Tutankhamen's tomb is the smallest royal tomb found in the Valley of the Kings.

Riddles in Stone

The interiors of many royal tombs were decorated with pictures and signs. For important records, the ancient Egyptians wrote in a language of picture words called **hieroglyphs.** Student scribes took years to memorize the hundreds of hieroglyphic signs.

For centuries, archaeologists could not decode the strange picture symbols that seemed to make up the pyramid texts. It wasn't until 1799 that French soldiers accidentally discovered a code-breaker stone known as the Rosetta Stone. Using this stone, people were at last able to decipher the hieroglyphs and make sense of the ancient Egyptian language.

M
Owl

| Man | T Bread | N Water | Arm | I, E, Y Reed | Mouth | K Basket |

The Rosetta Stone has three kinds of ancient writing on it. The upper section is in hieroglyphs. The midsection is a form of **demotic script** used for everyday writing in ancient Egypt. The lower section is in Greek. In 1822, after years of work, French scholar Jean-François Champollion finally began to understand the meaning of the writing on the Rosetta Stone.

The ancient Egyptians invented the world's first paper by using stems of the papyrus reed.

An Ancient Art

Ancient Egyptian artists painted picture stories on the vast walls of tombs and the towering pillars of temples. Teams of artists worked by candlelight in the dark tombs. They used pigments made from crushed rocks and minerals mixed with egg whites and tree gum. Brilliant shades of green came from powdered malachite and deep reds came from iron oxides. The colors in many of the temples and tombs are as vivid today as when they were first brushed on the walls more than 5,000 years ago.

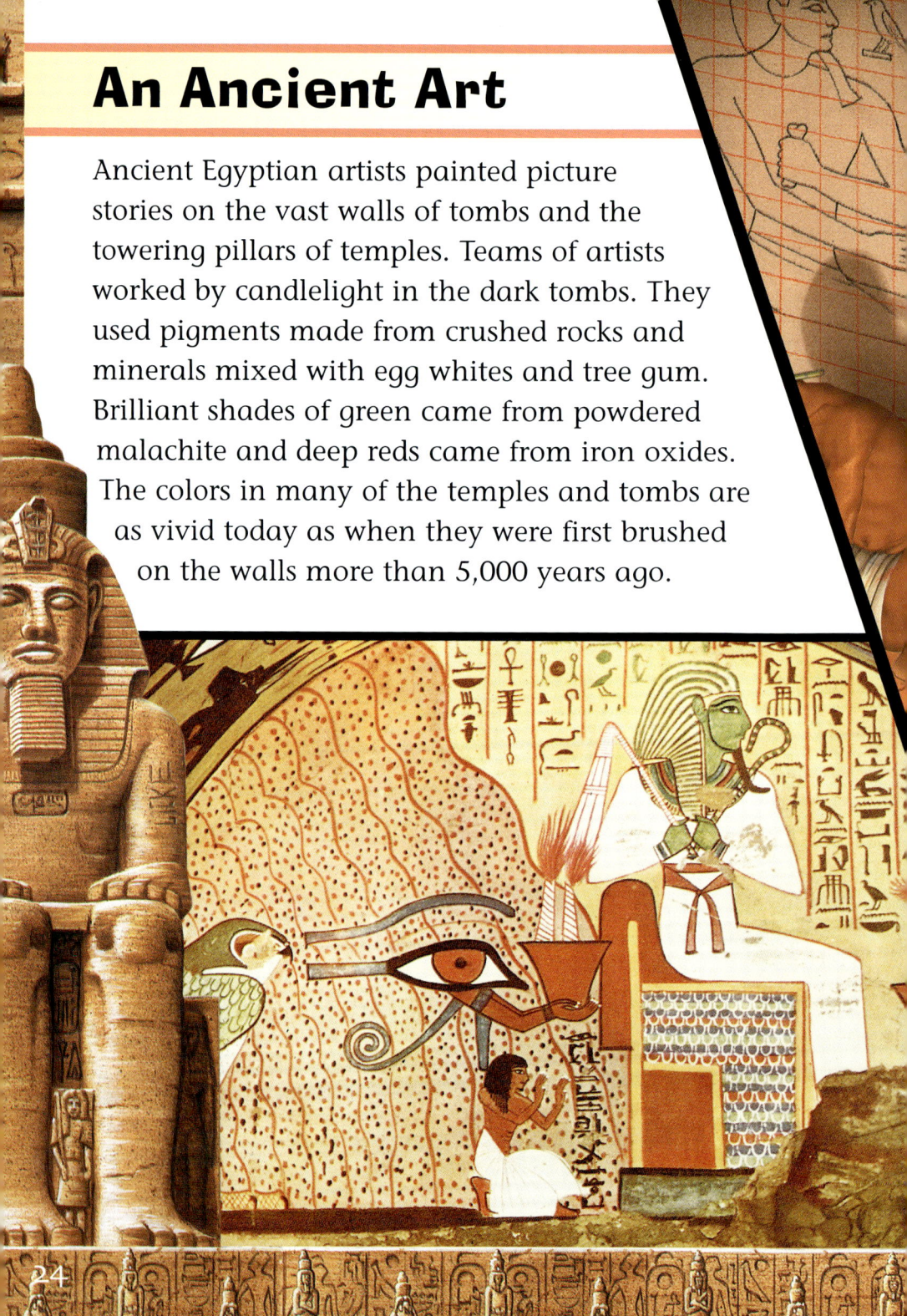

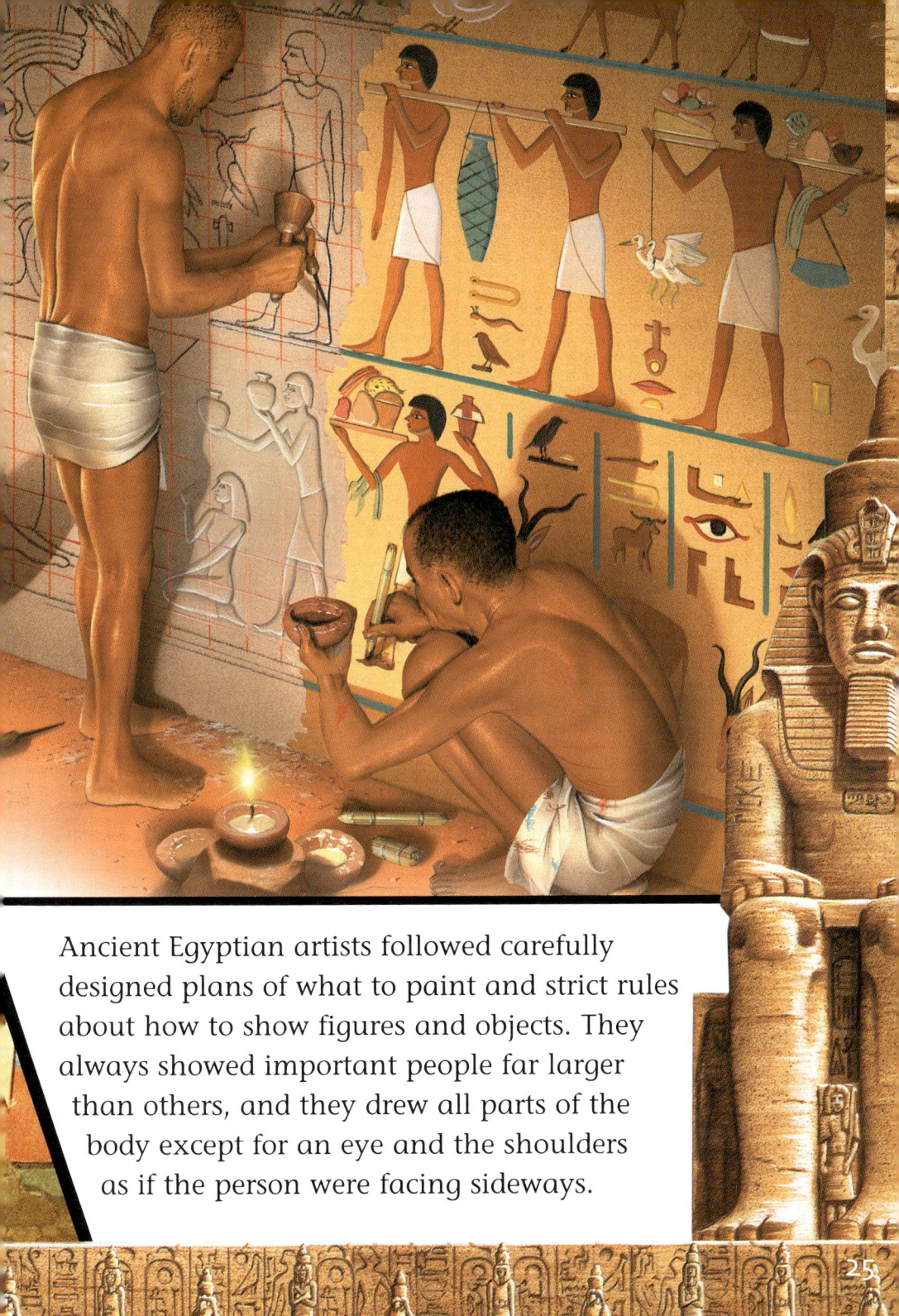

Ancient Egyptian artists followed carefully designed plans of what to paint and strict rules about how to show figures and objects. They always showed important people far larger than others, and they drew all parts of the body except for an eye and the shoulders as if the person were facing sideways.

Keeping the Past Alive

Over the centuries, archaeologists have come from near and far to uncover the hidden secrets of Egypt's past. There have been many great **excavations** and many dazzling discoveries. Grand statues, mysterious mummies, and gleaming jewels are displayed in the museums of Egypt and around the world. In Egypt, expert restorers protect statues, pyramids, and tomb walls, repairing damage caused by time and weather. By studying these treasures from the past, people today can learn about the customs and beliefs of this great nation of people who lived on Earth so long ago.

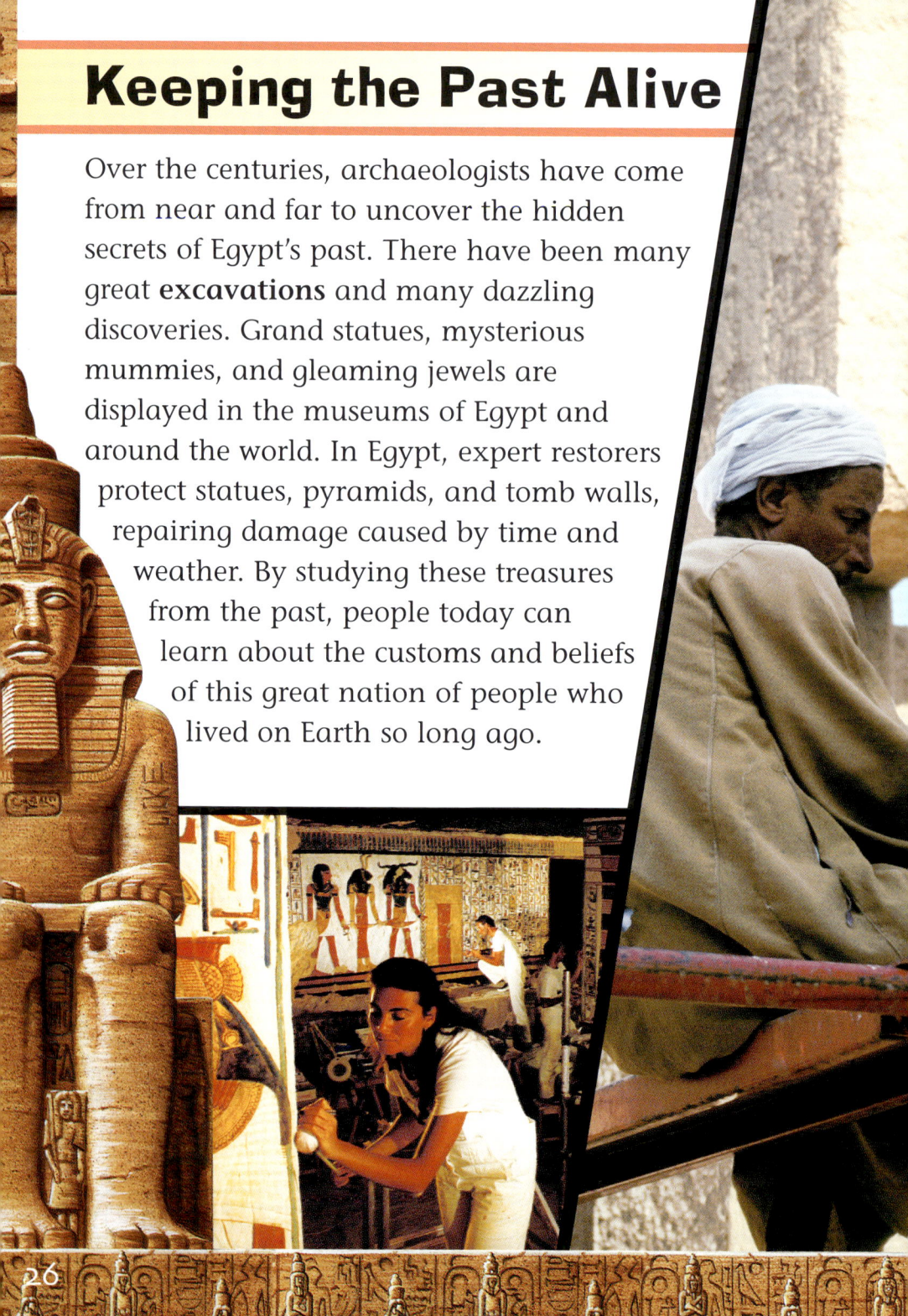

When the Aswan Dam was built across the River Nile in the 1960s, it created a lake. Many of the monuments and temples were moved to prevent them from being flooded.

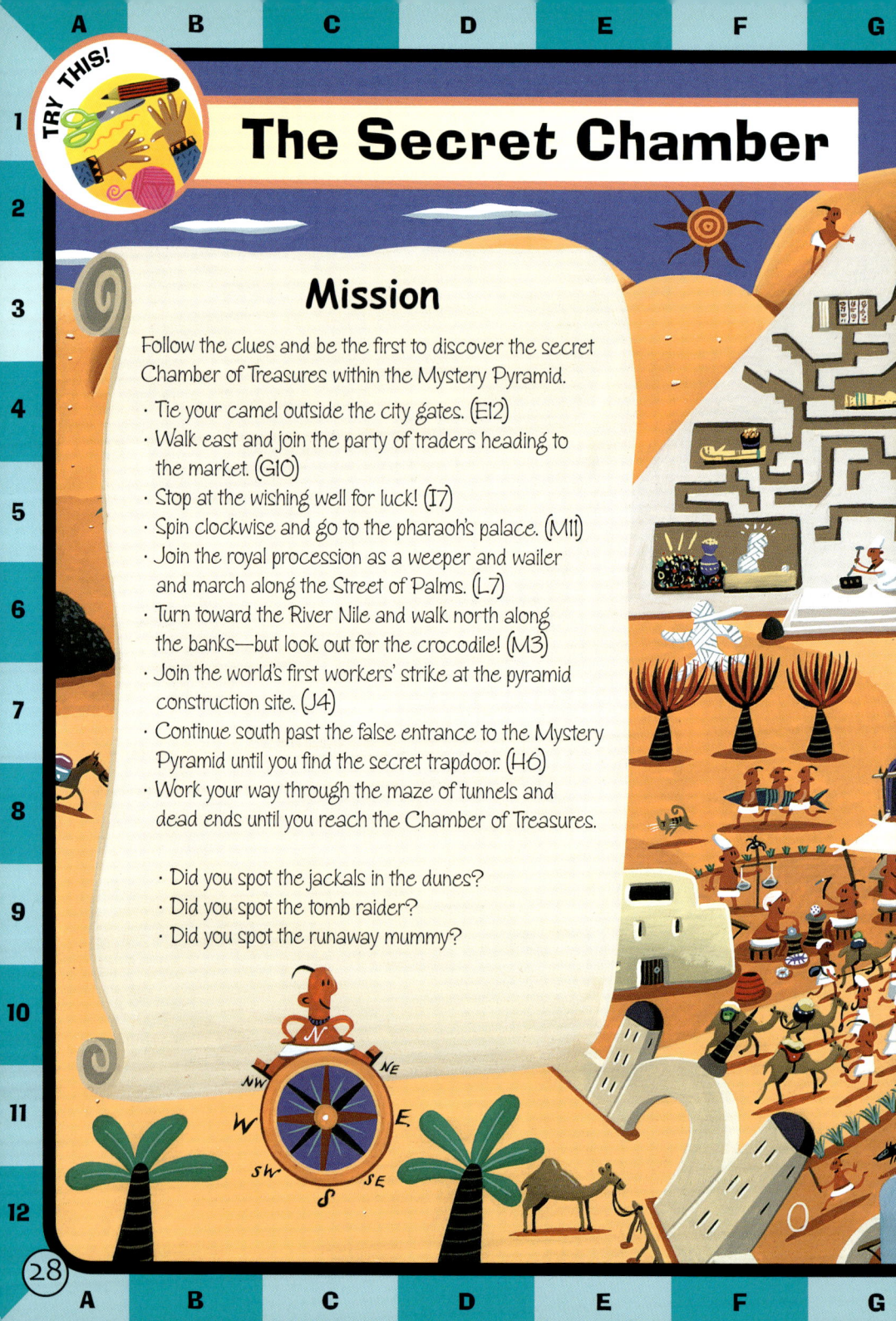

Glossary

canopic jars – small jars for storing the organs of a dead person when the body was mummified

civilization – an organized society that has developed customs, government, technology, and the arts

demotic script – a common form of ancient Egyptian writing used by scribes that was faster than forming hieroglyphs. This script was written from right to left.

dynasty – a series of rulers who belong to the same family

Egyptologist – an archaeologist who finds out how people lived in ancient Egypt by studying the things they left behind

embalmer – a person who treats a dead body to prevent its decay. Ancient Egyptian embalmers used spices and oils.

excavation – an area of land that has been dug up by archaeologists to expose objects from the past

hieroglyphs – the symbols and pictures of ancient Egyptian writing. Some hieroglyphs were used as symbols for both objects and letters or sounds.

natron – a salt from the desert that absorbs moisture

pharaoh – a ruler of ancient Egypt. The title comes from the ancient Egyptian word *per-ao,* meaning "the great house."

sarcophagi – the plural form of sarcophagus, which is a large stone box that protected a mummy's coffin

Index

archaeology	17, 26
bazaars	10–11
Cairo	13, 16
cats	19
fashion	10
food	11
Giza	12–13
grave robbers	20–21
hieroglyphs	22–23
language	22–23
mummies	16–20, 28
pharaohs	6–9, 12, 14–16, 20–21
pyramids	12–15, 20–21, 26
River Nile	4–5, 27
Rosetta Stone	22–23
society	9
sphinx	12
tombs	12, 17–18, 20–22, 24, 26
tourism	13
Tutankhamen, King	20–21

Research Starters

1. The ancient Greek historian Herodotus called Egypt "the gift of the Nile." Why do you think he said this? What can you find out about modern Egypt and how the River Nile is used today?

2. The Old Kingdom is also known as the Pyramid Age because it was during this time that Egypt's massive pyramids were constructed. Research how long the three Kingdoms of ancient Egypt lasted, and find out how the Roman Empire conquered ancient Egypt.

3. Egypt is not the only ancient civilization that built pyramids. Discover where in the world other pyramids were constructed and how these compare and contrast with the pyramids of ancient Egypt.

4. Mummies have been discovered in several parts of the world. Find out where and research how scientists today use technology to study mummies without unwrapping them.